Adicktion

12 Steps to Me

TERRA V RILEY

Table of Contents

aDicktion

One of the first books I remember reading is from the famous collection Fun with Dick & Jane.

Look, Jane.

Look, look.

See, Dick.

See, see.

Oh, see Dick.

Dick: The person place or thing that prevents you from being the best version of you.

While in discussion with one of my mentees, this inspiration was born, and now it is time for it to grow.

We all have a Dick or two that have caused us an issue along the way. When it gets to the point of "or two," we can see the beginning of a pattern. By Dick, four consider yourself adDICKted.

Let's break that! To live the abundantly full life, you deserve you must develop a sustainable plan of self-care.

After years of mismanaged relationships, I discovered the first mismanaged relationship in my life was the root of all the others. We mismanage our relationship with SELF.

This book came to mind with this thought, as little girls, we are encouraged to chase Dick. We chase Jack up the hill fall and break our crown. Some childhood stories encourage us to be helpless and wait for rescue. Who just sits in a tower waiting on an ogre?

I am no psychiatric expert or behavior specialist, but life has taught me some valuable lessons worth sharing.

Breaking my aDicktion is a process, and I am grateful I allow the spirit within to take me through. Nothing about it was   or is easy. There are still moments of growth that hurt in the best way. In this book, we will explore the 12 steps to Break aDicktion.

- Admit you are an aDickt
- Resist Dick
- Change your routine
- Disconnect from shared situations
- Rekindle your relationship with you!
- Set Short- and Long-term goals
- Develop a hidden talent
- Commit to a cause

- Increase spirituality
- Increase financial stability
- Be charitable with wisdom.
- Make no apology for choosing You.

Chapter 1: ADMIT It!

∞

Proverbs28:13

He who conceals his transgressions will not prosper. But he who confesses and forsakes them will find compassion.

∞

We are all aware the first step to recovery is admitting it. This scripture tells us hiding it prevents us from growing. Just acknowledging it, saying it out loud allows you to find compassion. Trust that you are not in this alone. Someone walked in these shoes before you.

Late teens early 20's my girls, and I regularly used the phrase, "Dick Dumb." Don't get me wrong there is nothing wrong with a stable relationship, so do not confuse any of this for man hate or bashing. Acknowledging is empowerment if you let it empower you. Dick Dumb is a thing, and it must be defined, so you know the signs. Dick Dumb is The abandonment of self for a relationship void of future guarantee.

Every Friday for as many years as you have been friends, you all have had a standing Friday situation. Now that Lola is dating Rico, she has started missing Fridays. A couple of times, OK, understandable, we all have lives. This weekend is Homecoming, and the whole city is lit. Your crew is well known, and if anybody is going to be in the VIP, it is your crew. We made the plan. Everything is a go. You all have arranged a suite, limo transportation, and VIP accommodations at all the events. Friday comes, and Lola is coming with Rico. However, Rico has just arrived with his boys and no Lola. No doubt, the whip is pulling up, and the crew is headed straight to Lola. Arriving, the crew finds Lola sulking, drinking wine, and a hot mess. All Girl Magic pulls sis together. Couple shots a puff & pass later, Lola begins to talk herself out of the foolish behavior she was classifying as loyalty.

If we are honest, we all have been Dick Dumb at some point. Maybe your Dick is a job that limits you. Dick can be the schedule of activities you keep that still does not fill the void.

Dick Dumb is like sitting by an embalmed body on a ventilator and expecting to have signs of life. Living Dick Dumb makes you the body looking at the body. You have got to grasp breath before you die. You cannot keep holding your breath and expect to live.

Holding your breath is allowing or waiting on people places or things to determine your level of life and not taking control of yourself. Being in a relationship with anyone or anything requires an understanding of mutual responsibility.

My Theory of Reciprocal Responsibility states that we are both responsible for the life of the relationship. This theory operates by this formula, Add to Life + Correct Life + Protect Life= Beneficial Relationship. When my Pastor Daddy William L. Brown taught that lesson, I felt it!

To move like this, you must have yourself together somewhat. Yes, it is crucial to have you together before any type of relationship can be beneficial. You must give what you expect to get.

Admitting your ADICKtion is the only way to begin restructuring relationships in your life.

Admitting that we misplace responsibility for personal happiness is a great start. We expect too much from outside sources. No one person on earth can make you happy. Even Mr. Perfect has imperfect moments. In his moment of imperfection immediately, the emotional response is relationship crisis mode. Too much sis, he is human and subject to error just like you. At this moment, you very well might be in the wrong. Learning to admit wrongs helps to break ADICKtion.

All of us know someone that feels trapped in a dead-end job.

Day after day, they repeat the same complaints but never prepare for change. Staying for the pay, benefits, or time on the job is ADICKtion. Admitting this is alarming for some people. Exposing it frees you to endless possibilities. You can never invest wrong when the investment is you. Identify the area of ADICKtion and admit it—step 1 to the break.

Chapter 2: Resist Dick

You must stay in your home, ma'am.
Dick is NOT considered essential.

James 4:7

Submit to God. Resist the devil, and he will run from you.

We spend a lot of time committing ourselves to relationships that do not benefit us. We spend even more time resisting

God. Learn to submit to God, be open to him. Learning to shut the devil out or the improper influences out will be the greatest reward on our road to recovery

We have a power within that causes the things contrary to the Godly progression of our lives to be dismissed called submission. Typically, when we talk of submission, there is a little tension. Who just wants to bow down to what someone else says to do?

As I am writing this, we are amid COVID19, a Global Pandemic, and now the USA is quarantined. We are in quarantine with increased orders for public safety. Our new way of life is Social Distancing. The rules are required to increase because of people's resistance to submit to the request. Submission can save your life.

Submission displays many things about your character. It shows you as a willing learner. It is like a badge of honor, and it is not awful. When I submit to the rules of a teacher, for example, I am in the best position to receive the lesson prepared for me. I can learn, and apply the experience, because I have submitted to the fact that this person is knowledgeable of the subject, and able to present it in a form I can understand. Submission to God places us in position for HIS will to be accomplished in us.

Anything that does not push you toward becoming the best version of yourself is no good for you. Even though the relationship may offer you a certain excitement, with a hint of risqué, which appeals to our need for a lustful adventure, it is naturally and spiritually no good. I am sure you have heard and maybe said, you can't tell your heart who to love. Looking back, can you see this phrase is simply an excuse to stay in nonproductive situations. To get to the best part of you, resistance to everything that causes you to settle or compromise is essential. You must know the stoppers and blockers and avoid them at all costs.

Social media plays such a significant part in our lives. We connect on various platforms for a variety of purposes. Some may start with the purest of intentions; however, the messaging factor kicks in. Good Morning Beautiful! Hey stranger. What it do sexy? All little intro phrases that soon lead to an ongoing textlationship with Dick. See Dick, See Dick text. Where is Dick? Why hasn't Dick text? Now, this texting situation has become part of your routine. Communication is where it all starts. Having a mature and concrete position on how you deal with social media is vital. Immaturity will allow us and often push us to entertain the inbox, Dick. We foster faux feelings so long until they become a faux reality7. Resisting Dick begins with first knowing how to resist yourself. Self - control is life-saving. Self- Control is sexy. I teach my mentor group S.H.E. Sisterhood Excellence, it is crucial ten years after you graduate to continue to appear on the fellas hit list. That is the list they wished and never stopped fantasizing they hit. Yes, just like that because everything in their circle of influence is telling them to whore out it is your right Sis Do You.

Not so, and I cannot claim any type of real Sister-Pride if I allowed them to be miseducated or misinformed. Do not let social media with a side of lonely get you stuck in a tough situation with a crazy Dick.

The purpose God has for your life has no room for purposeless conversation.

Resisting the urge just to shoot a text is something you will fight with for a little bit. I know this because, on occasion, I must remind myself how he is doing is not my business. We are natural nurturers. As women, we feel the responsibility of caring for everyone and fixing everything. Sis let me free you. You cannot take care of everybody unless you first take care of you. Take care of Yourself in every aspect of you. Fixing everything can never be all on you. Let's face it, none of us are that brilliant. I intensely read the Serenity Prayer one day, my favorite part is help me to accept the things I cannot change. Acceptance is a way of life. Accepting it means I receive this, or I welcome this. I am at peace with the things I cannot change, and I am moving on. In the stage of resisting, we must be at peace with not having what is familiar. Now let me drop this so we can move on, Dick is not always the Devil.

Sometimes that Dick is you. Oh, indeed, you can be your worst, Dick. You see all the traits of Pretty Tony, and you just going to drag us off into this? Again, you can be your own worst Dick. Resist your devils, and they will run. Resist comparing people and situations to what happened before. Trust yourself to make the right decisions and make them.

Chapter 3: Change your routine

Normality is a paved road: its comfortable to walk. But no flowers grow on it. Vincent Van Gogh

Everything must change; nothing can stay the same. To experience life outside of aDicktion; you must create a new routine.

Resale shopping has become more popular than ever. Online shopping has replaced a lot of the time we once spent in stores. Take a moment to think about your closet. We all have a blouse, a pair of pants, maybe even a few dresses we have not worn and will not wear in years. There isn't room for more and certainly no need for more when there are items that still have tags. When your girl turned you on to her little consignment shop, she set you on a path that would soon prove ADicktive.

Resale stores have a marketing game that requires no fliers, only a schedule and Color of the Day Sales. You have memorized the table and have made it your daily thing to stop in after work to see what they have. First, it is one store every other Saturday until it's 2, 3, 4. The aDicktion is getting so real you're heading out of town to find resale stores. That Saturday has turned into every day.

We think we are saving by shopping cheap. You may be defeating the savings by buying every day. Change the routine. Dick, the retail store, is holding you hostage to a false sense of saving when you are needlessly stockpiling stuff. Stockpiling stuff quickly spills off into other areas of our lives. We hold on to and collect people that give us the comfortable feel of friendship, and it is one-sided. Houses hold us hostage to memories and lost hope of what could have been. You will not move because that is where it all began. If it is finished, let it go.

Change the routine of comfortable and relaxed. Change encounters resistance. It is giving in to change for the better will bless your life. Embrace change for the better and allow yourself to grow.

Chapter 4:

Disconnect From Shared Situations

Amos 3:3 How can two walk together unless they agree?

All his friends are not your friends, and your friends are not his friends. Let go of the things that tied the relationship together.

Let go of that job that does not appreciate you. Continuing to dwell in shared situations does not contribute to your freedom. This behavior is a continuation of your bondage.

The Number You Have Reached....

Mr. telephone man, there's something wrong with my line when I dialed my baby's number. I got a click every time. Mr. telephone man, something's wrong with my line. New Edition

Remember when we used landlines? I can remember having a personal phone line, and as a result of irresponsibility, my mom had

15

it disconnected. It was so embarrassing for my friends to say, "your number is disconnected." No joke. Let's compare our connections to things and people in our lives as landlines; we must disconnect from some callers. You cannot afford unprofitably.

As a couple, you will develop mutual friends. That is a good thing and a bad thing at the same time. Mutual friends are suitable for the development of the social aspect of your relationship. However, I am a firm believer that every woman must maintain her circle outside the couple.

Bryan and Kathy are our mutual friend couple. Bryan and Boo went to college together, and Kathy and Boo work together. I know them because of Boo and Kathy, and I have gotten close. I spend a lot of time with Kathy because the guys are best friends. Now the time has passed, and Boo and I are not doing so well. Kathy and Bryan have no obligation to me. They are obligated to each other and Boo. Me trying to maintain a friendship with Kathy puts me in position to still Boo stalk. Not meaning to hurt me, Kathy shares all she knows going on in Boo's situation. Me being aDickted, I listen and internalize the information. Kathy sharing Boo's information begins to create blockers for me to move on. I find myself envisioning what he is doing and why he could not do it with me. Removing myself from the common familiar of Bryan and Kathy strengthens me. Maintaining my circle gives me a place to heal and be encouraged by my friends with no attachment to Boo.

Why keep going to the same places that stir up the feelings of missing him? What is the benefit of continually draining yourself emotionally? Disconnect contact. It is going to be hard, but it's going to be worth it. You will feel the benefits of disconnection early if you allow the process to begin. Trust yourself to be alright in new surroundings and routines.

Chapter 5:

Rekindle with yourself. Me Myself and I

Mark 6:31

Then, because so many people were coming and going that they did not even have a chance to eat, he said to them, "Come with me, by yourselves to a quiet place and get some rest".

You should not live a life of extreme exhaustion. Nowhere is it written that you must work your fingers to the bone. If you give out all of you, what will you have left?

When I got married, everything in my life became about him. The worst mistake ever. I abandoned my friendships and activities to please him. Even in doing this, it was not enough. No matter how many changes or compromises I made, it was never good enough.

I based this choice on what I thought would help my marriage unify. Being 1 is such a complicated and often confusing concept. The oneness of marriage is the unity of the two in matters concerning the health, growth, and development of the established unit called family. Harmony does not mean all my friends are his friends. It is not a dictatorship. He proved this every time he went out, and I stayed home thinking he was just making a quick run. It is okay, laugh, call me stupid because we have all done it.

In these lonely home moments, I began to journal and talk to God. Embarrassment prevented me from talking to friends. Hurt would not allow me to mention a thing to family. Guess what they knew. Knowing that they knew sent me into a state of depression, regret, and a whole lot of places, I had no business residing. Dr. Laura A. Brown, my spiritual mom, and author of The They Effect, teaches a very life forming lesson on emotions. The general concept is this, "Your emotions belong to you. If you own them, control them by bringing them into the captivity of Holy Spirit". In other words, the power of Holy Spirit in me is more significant than anything happening outside of me. I can release my power or relinquish my control. I choose to release it. Releasing the power of Holy Spirit strengthens you by shifting the atmosphere. Too deep? When you positively charge your surroundings with strong, affirming words and attitude, that is the energy that surrounds you. In good soil, good crops grow.

Me is the publicly accessible part of Myself, which is the reasoning and planning center between me and I. I am who and what I am with no apology. Me, Myself, I'm still building I.

Me is the part of you people say they know. They know the part that becomes an ADickt.

If we think of ourselves, 3ply Me would be the outer layer that the people see.

Myself is the inner layer. The inner layer is where my emotions, my understanding, my hopes, my love, etc. all things genuine reside in the inner layer. I is the core of Me, Myself, and I. I am firm and secure in the center. I am at peace in the heart. My most sacred relationships and beliefs receive nurture in my core. My heart is the place of firm resolution and sound decision. It is the essence of me.

How many times have you heard a person say I know her? Or you have heard someone say that's not even like him? This statement would indicate that a person knows the real character of the person of whom they speak. My children can say to one another quickly, mom said, or mom would say because they know my voice. They see the character in which I speak. This exchange happens because they are privileged as my children to recognize me myself, and I.

Facebook friends can say they know you or know of you. But unless there is a personal connection, they cannot perceive your character and demeanor in its true essence.

Myself is the intimate part of me reserved for me. It is the liaison between myself and I. Myself is where I determine my goals, my dreams, and visions. Never allow anyone to make you feel guilty for having an extraordinary idea. It is the dreamers that make things happen in our society. No matter how big or small your dream, do not be afraid to make it your reality.

Taking small steps is the beginning of walking the long walk. The long walk is that walk of success. It leads you to doors that were once closed. The long walk places you before the very people others would not believe had time for you. There is a scripture that encourages us not to grow weary in well-doing there is a reward if we don't faint. It is important to align myself with individuals who will help me to attain my goals. Be cautious of dream smashers and vision blasters. These are the people that come into your life and tell you what you dream of is impossible. They are the ones that tell you your visions are foolish.

Myself has no business with these types of people. Their energy is poisonous to I and me. I is the absolute of me. When I think of the I portion of myself, I think of the I am statement of God. I am that I am that I am. I am a woman feminine and proud to be. I am human with feelings and emotions that have value and merit. God created me fearfully and wonderfully in His image. My, I am statement allows me to act in the power of God given to me according to what I believe. It is in the eye of me that I create and walk into the predestined place God prepared for me. I do not apologize for living in the God moment. I will not accept anything less than what God has intended for me. I will not compromise anymore. This day I resolve that I am worth it. I determined I can have it.

It is my earnest belief that if I humble myself before God, he will exalt me meaning he will lift me when I am low. My relationship with God centers me. And our relationship Trinity to trinity is all that matters. It is my place of worship. I is my place of peace absolute peace. 16

Beyoncé performs a song Me Myself and I. Most people would not look at it as a motivational song or as a song to take you into praise, but for me, that song does it. After all, you have been through what a blessed assurance to know that that relationship created with God in the I will keep you and sustain you when all else fails.

Chapter 6:

Set short- and long-term goals.

Proverbs 21:5

The plans of the diligent lead to profit.

Be a goal digger, dream chaser, an accomplishment seeking individual. In doing this, you will find a brand new you. Be a goal digger, a goal setter, and a go-getter. Be all that you can be. Take this time to evaluate your life. Look at the things that are versus the things that can be. Notice I did not say look at the past, there is nothing we can do about that now. Never beat yourself up about what happened before. Give thanks that you are no longer in that situation, rejoice and live fully.

Looking at it outside of the context of a relationship, I often think of my musical career. People do not take into consideration how it makes me feel when they ask, why don't you have an album? Or why are you still here and not somewhere making lots of money? They don't mean any harm. Thinking they are encouraging you, never realize how much they may have damaged you. Eight years ago, I took a trip to St Louis Mo to audition for Sunday's Best the BET

Gospel talent show. My expectation was never really to be a gospel performer; however, I wanted to share my gift with the world. While in Saint Louis, the dream girls and I fulfilled our dream of eating at Sweetie Pies. We even met some of the cast of the reality show. After being up half the night, waiting through numerous auditions, my body and spirit became worn. The Dream girls informed me that Ihad not been eliminated. My number crossed the screen for the next round. Which was the final round to the judges. Looking back, I can give you several reasons why we got in the car and came home.

Being honest and transparent fear drove me home. We often sabotage our accomplishments by allowing fear to overwhelm our faith. The past performance was not the first time that I had graced a national platform. Five years before this, I participated in the Inspiration Network CATS (Christian Artist Talent Search). Participation in that competition, I believe, rebirthed a fear of rejection. I knew for sure my presentation and content were the best presented; however, my packaging was all off. I have shared this to encourage you. Fear will keep you broken and in bondage. The only fear that will reward you is the fear of God. Not an afraid type fear, but a fear of missing your blessing. I fear not pleasing God with the gifts and talents he has blessed me with. That is why it is important to me that this book be a success. If it reaches one person and changes her life, I have done My job.

Writing the vision and making it understandable is more than scripture. It is a way of life. Before you embark upon any endeavor, you should always have a clear plan. Before you set your plan make sure it aligns with the plan of God for your life. Following the plan of God is like passing the abilities test. If Terra can follow this and get it, I can trust her with her own vision. I believe that's how Abba Father deals with me.

Short term goals are the things that you can accomplish within 30 to 60 days. Your long-time goal should coincide with the short-term goal, but it will take an extended amount of time to achieve. For example, I am a singer, so recording is no issue for me. Pulling all the material together and putting it in a finished package has been the issue.

My short-term goal was to collect all material. Long term goal is to put together a collection of every piece of work that I have done so that my children will have wealth far beyond my days. Years ago, I remembered sitting at a table paying a lot of money for a three-ring binder, some crayons, and a glue stick thinking that this was going to fix my life. It was not until I did as God told me, WRITE the vision I made it plain so that those who see it would run with it, did I begin to see things align. Yes, the idea has lingered for a while and suffered a few setbacks and delays. But now I am at the threshold of the vision coming to reality. The vision could only come to reality when I first acknowledged and obeyed the vision of God. Without resistance I have learned to move according to the spirit and not what I see. He promised to watch over his word, and it would accomplish the goal. When we delight ourselves in the vision of God for our lives, he gives us the desires of our heart. Set your goal and commit them to God.

The key to successful goal accomplishment is commitment. We commit to all the wrong things and willfully slack when it comes to committing to ourselves. Willful slacking is a tactic of sabotage. A direct result of fear. Before you get started on your next short-term goal, I would like for you to commit to the following.

1. If I start it, I must finish it. As a crafter, I have a lot of starts and stop projects around the house. Not often do I return to the start and stop plans to complete them. Until recently, I began to look at the start and stop projects as wasted time and energy. To be successful, I cannot be wasteful. If I start, I must complete no matter how long it takes; I must complete

it. Sometimes this requires accountability. Trust someone to hold you accountable for completing your project.

2. Never take on more than I can handle. My aunt has always told me never to jump into anything you cannot complete yourself. My aunt's advice is a good rule of thumb for me because I like things done a certain way. Relying on others to do things how I want them done does not always work out. If people should happen to walk away from the project, I don't get upset anymore because I have made plans to complete it with or without.

3. Give yourself a chance to fail and recover. Failure and recovery are the ultimate teaching guides of goal setting. You can only fail if you don't try. That means you're working at something. Recovering from a failure places tools in your toolbox to help you continue building towards your goal. You don't have to fear failure ever again once you've gone through this process. You have experience with failure and understand that it is not the death of your dream or goal. It is an opportunity for you to resuscitate the idea. Bring it back to life.

4. Allow no one to say you can't. Be bold in your no statement. No, you may not tell me no. No, you may not suggest that I. No, you may not offer. There are people in your life that you

know for sure their suggestions and offers to help seem questionable. Even the inquiry, how are you, is more of a setup than a step up. Be bold in your no. Protect that that is precious to you. Your dream, your vision, and goal are the essences of you. Protect that, allow no one to say that you cannot achieve your dream.

5. Just do it! This famous slogan will resound for years. Just do it. Whatever it is, just do it. You have the ability, capability, mobility, and strength to endure; just do it! Surround yourself with people who will cheer for you. Enjoy the company of those that celebrate and not tolerate you. Every championship team needs an active fan base. Individuals are waiting to cheer you on. They believe in you. They are excited for you. They are waiting for you just to do it.

I am a spades player. Pretty good if I must say so myself. I'm amazing however, when playing with my best friend. People hate to see us sit at the table together. Our trash-talking game is superb. Our country dumb is very deceiving. And the Spade break, oh, it is legendary. I am big on comparisons so; I compare life to spades. Sure, we all want face cards and all the highest in every suit. What do you do when you get numbers? How do you handle the hand you receive? Well, the right partner first off can read your hand. With proper play, and support what looked like a bad hand on its own can turn into somebody's rise and fly.

Let's use a job as a dick in our life. The goal is to get away from this awful job. Why do I want to leave this job? Because I am not happy. Why am I not happy at my job? Because I do not feel appreciated. Why do I not feel valued? Because no one ever rewards my excellent work. Why do I continue to give my best? Because I am passionate about my career. Why have I not applied for the same position somewhere else? Because I have been here for years, and I am afraid of losing my seniority.

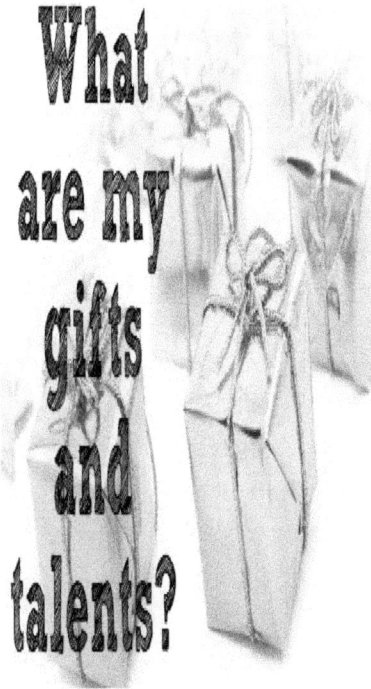

What are my gifts and talents?

Asking 5 Whys, you will discover the root cause of why you are still stuck with Dick. Take a moment and ask yourself five whys concerning the dick in your life. Getting over it is a series of questions as well. Who what when where how and why? If you had an excellent English teacher, none of this should be foreign to you. If not, let me introduce you to a simple process of problem-solving. You can apply these questions to any situation.

Chapter 7:

Discover Your Hidden Talents

I can honestly say that God gifted me in many areas. Sometimes I am amazed at the things I can do. I am not bragging because sometimes it's out of necessity that I have discovered my abilities. As a child, I lived in my own child celebrity. At a very young age, I performed for former Atlanta mayor Andrew Young in Niagara Falls, NY. The opportunity was significant. Again, I sang before Jesse Jackson during his campaign for president another big feat. I also led worship with From the Heart International Ministries Praise and Worship Team under the late Dr. John Cherry. BET and INSP, been on there. The ultimate is anytime I am in the presence of my Favorites The Clark Sisters. I have even blessed to spend time in production with the great Vickie Winans. The list of musical accomplishments could go on, and despite all of these, I still had a fear. I feared public rejection. I felt no one would appreciate my music and that it was only good enough for the people in my circle.

My mother, Pastor Carolyn Wilkins, is one of the most excellent musicians I know. I learned on the bench of her upright piano. There wasn't a three-part harmony I did not know because my mother had drilled them in my head. Looking back at the time spent learning from her, I understand now that I was receiving my portion of her. I cherish this gift given to me by my mother. Her wisdom understood a uniqueness early in my voice. She always made it a point to have me in the best places to hear the best music. She guarded my gift close and allowed nothing to pervert the anointing upon my life. I am grateful that my mom did not let the lure of fortune or fame persuade her to pimp my gifts. No, not at all! Quite the contrary. It is because my mom guarded my gift, someone like R. Kelly never got a chance to pee on me.

I love crafting, and that is a gift I share with my Aunt Carmen. The comedian in me, many credit my father. For over 30 years, I have learned to deal with his absence and honor his name by being everything he would want me to be, which is what I would want to be myself.

Within me, something was dying to get out. So big it scared me. During quarantine, a spiritual revelation came to me. God had to require me to stand still for me to see that he is God naturally. It is in quarantine that God began to remind me of the things that he placed inside me. All the fears that I possessed thinking what people would say, he showed me during this time they, the people are not around anyway. Getting free from the opinions and stepping into the reality of this blessing has been such a lifted burden. I am stirring up every gift within me, and I suggest you do the same. If your talent is making smoothies, then do that. If your offering is reading bedtime stories, do that. If your gift is smiling at seniors and encouraging them be an encourager, everything about you is essential.

In the face of the pandemic of 2020 COVID-19, I have learned some things. The term essential and nonessential has made me look at life differently. We want to place a high value on individuals with a lot of money. During COVID-19, wealth alone could not make you essential Those considered to be the lowliest workers among us became the most critical.

Grocery store clerks are now frontline workers, and I am grateful for them as I have been. Gas station attendants are now frontline workers.

People who we once considered to work less important jobs are now the very people we depend on. What's not essential is all the lines that we have waiting on the new Jordan's. Overcrowded malls and shopping centers are not vital. And spending an entire day in the salon is unnecessary! Quarantine has taught us that being next in line for a pedicure or manicure is nonessential. During quarantine, we all are presented with a unique opportunity to discover a hidden talent.

There are a lot of things I know I can do and plenty of things I want to do. My eye game has always been keen, and since a little girl, I have had a fixation with a sewing machine. I've never learned to use one seriously. I've always admired people who could knit or crochet. So, during this time, my daughter and I are learning to knit and crochet. I wanted to teach her about discovering a hidden talent. Not only is she learning to knit, but she is writing a book as well. She is ten years old, and I feel that it is important to teach her now coping mechanisms that will not only help her stay mentally healthy, but also bring her wealth.

There are many things within you that you have just dismissed well now is as good a time as any to make it happen. Decorate that room, paint that dresser, and trim the window in wallpaper. As the song says, it's your thing, do what you want to do. Create moments that make you smile. The discovery of new and exciting parts of yourself will not only create a smile momentarily; it will imprint a smile upon your heart. Allow your heart to smile; it deserves it. If we are fair, our hearts endure a lot. They suffer attack time and time again, yet they keep beating. Broken numerous times, yet they keep pumping. Abandoned and left for dead, yet they survive. Going within your spirit and freeing yourself to discover the hidden parts of you will bless everyone around you if you just let it be. Sometimes we must apologize to the world for cheating it of the best version of us. We have so much to offer, but we refrained in fear. We have amazing ideas, but we don't share them because of fear. Let's redefine fear so that it no longer holds us back, but it empowers us.

Fear

F forget what people think or say

E expect the best

A assure yourself God is with you.

R rejoice, your reward is on the way.

Every day, encourage yourself, you can, will and shall no matter what. Fear is Fuel when you've been Bossed Up by God!

Chapter 8: Commit to A Cause

Luke 6:38

Give, and it shall be given to you good measure pressed down, shaken together and running over shall men give into your bosom. With the same standard, you provide it will return to you.

There is something within you dying to come out. Let it live. Let it live out loud.

I am a Para educator for the Lansing School District. When I started my job, I had no clue about the ways it would change my life. My students have so significantly impacted my life. I prayed that I would be able to see a particular group graduate from high school. We are now in high school, and what an adventure. I take my job a little more seriously than the average person in my position. Maybe because my boys arrested my heart, they looked inside me and pulled out what they needed. In turn making me better in the gifts I had. And, I am developing new offerings. I am a champion for them. I will always make sure that they are acknowledged, not as a disabled part of society, but as a needed part of our community. My girls S.H.E restored a value in sisterhood that life circumstances had greatly damaged.

Autism is a Way of Love! #ASDGotMe These are some of my presentation openers when addressing students working with ASD students. The navigator program at my school pairs ASD students with non ASD students for social interaction and a little assistance in class. It was knowing that I will not tolerate the mistreatment of the ASD student, or the Gen ed student, that created a common bond between them that changes the situation from a class assignment, to a friendship. Seeing how this worked my cause became student advocacy.

I began to see that students no longer had a wealth of adults to rely on they had each other and needed guidance in handling peer to peer and adult relationships. The best teacher on how to deal with all people is a person with challenged abilities.

The level of patience and unselfishness I had to learn first as a parent, then as a paraeducator is beyond my imagined capabilities. It takes strength to not snap when your name is being called 500 times a day by 5 people. Not snapping came with understanding the assignment. Not only did these students need me I needed them. I tell them often they changed and saved my life. It's a true statement. I gained an ability to recognize academic and emotional challenges and it helped greatly with my parenting. Giving myself to something that I never knew would so immensely impact my life has been the best leap I ever took.

Committing to a cause outside your normal acts of charity and civic or religious duty is necessary for you to outgrow your aDicktion.

The energy you would continue to waste in one area is needed and wanted in another. I tell my students often, "If I am bothering you by caring for you please forgive me, the last thing I want to do is show you someone cares". The response after that statement has never failed. There is an immediate shift in the relationship and the doors are now open for effective mentorship.

Advocacy is a key component of mentorship. As you go through the process of breaking your aDicktion you will be able to effectively mentor others in aDicktive situations.

My job was the key to me getting back on my feet and finding value in my gifts, talents, and abilities. Committing to a cause greater than me with no expectation of reward or acknowledgment has been pivotal in my 12 steps to me.

Chapter 9: Increase Spirituality

Draw close to God, and God will Draw close to you.

James 4:8

Draw nigh to God, and he will draw nigh to you. Cleanse your hands of sin. Cleanse your heart, you double-minded.

There are things that we do, and we know they are wrong. These are the things that shame us from having a relationship with our creator; He sees all. God is not angry at us when we sin; He is just waiting for us to take advantage of the opportunity to be forgiven and to reunite in relationship with him. He doesn't want you to walk away; he's calling you closer.

Why is it that our intimate relationship with our creator is something people expect us to display? So they know it's real? We get caught up in Sanctified Lies trying to keep up the appearance of true salvation. We find ourselves caught between Dick and a hard place. Our emotions get all confused and we began to act outside ourselves. We become FAKE. New man arrives on the job, at the church, the gym wherever our hormones get to raging and things get to changing. Sometimes we get swept too soon and put everything out there for everyone to judge. You know how we do with them Me N Bae selfies after the first date? Posting 5 different pictures does not make the relationship real. All your miserable friends liking the pictures does not mean they are in true support of your relationship. I have a rule, you are not getting many likes on multiple men in the same year. I just can't with the recycle Bae Program.

Have you ever taken a selfie of you and God? What's the look on his face? Is he proud you are his lady? Or is he just dealing with the cheater? Drawing close to God is something that does not happen in a large crowd. It is a level of intimacy that you work on daily. It's meditating on good thoughts, righteous thoughts, selfless deeds, and communicating with him. God is not interested in our public performance. We've heard the statement freak in the sheets and a lady in the streets. God desires us to be intimate with him in our secret place and to be intimate with him in our public place. Our relationship with God will show up in how we live our lives daily. It is not based on church membership or attendance. Your relationship with God is not evident by how many auxiliaries you serve. It is evident in how you treat people. How you give reflects the evidence of God in your heart. Not how you tithe but how you give above and beyond the tithe.

Do you give without expectation, or are you a begrudging giver? Are you the giver that makes public announcements of what you've done? Giving for publicity is aDick for you and those you hold hostage.

When is the last time you laced God's ears with an ask for nothing praise? Praise gets God's attention. It causes heaven to listen to what you're saying. But worship is that intimate part. Worship is what causes God to get mushy and say yes. It delights him. We will spend more time trying to impress the flesh than we do in nurturing the spirit. Your soul has more value than your flesh. The flesh can sin and cause harm. The soul is the very heart of God breathed into man. Be honest, we all don't operate at our highest form of self at all times.

One of my favorite proverbs, a man without self- control is like a city without walls. Walls protect what is in a city, to keep out the enemy, to conceal what we have within our city, and to show the greatness and excellence of our buildings and wealth. It is vital that you maintain self-control and not allow yourself to become so thin that you have none of you left for you.

However, you believe it is fine with me; I am not afraid of people who think differently than I do. I embrace the knowledge of all religions, but I only subscribe to the spirit of living God within me, giving me the power to do great things on the earth. That is just me. Chanting meditating taking long walks just sitting by a pool of water can all be acts that draw you closer to God. Strangely enough, for me, it is my fish tanks. I have them everywhere I go because they are a constant reminder to me that he leads me beside still waters and that he always provides for me no matter what.

As I draw close to God, he draws close to me. There are some things that I can ask because of our relationship and receive without hesitation. Because of grace, I can live my best life and not be afraid to walk in abundance afforded me through Jesus Christ.

When we are pleasing to God, He will make our way prosperous. When we love him above everything and everyone, he will allow us the opportunity to experience Eros love. Eros love as he intended, no pain, no strain. Intimacy does not begin, nor does it end in the bedroom. Your first place of affection must be in prayer. A man goes hard for a woman on her knees praying for him way harder than they go for a woman just on her knees for him. How do you think the creator feels when we place everything and everyone above him?

Alone in your presence, it's just me and you here in this moment I'm focused only on you. You are the potter I am the clay mold me make me have your way. I want to be one with you. I want to be one with you here in your presence make me one with you.

Lyrics from 1 with You by Terra Riley

Chapter 10: Increase in Financial Stability

"Get your money in loaves, not slices" Nene Leakes, RHOA.

Ecclesiastes 10:19

A party gives laughter, wine gives happiness, and money answers everything.

Wisdom to obtain money is something that we all need. As you discover new freedoms in your emotions and your mind, you will find yourself creating new streams of income. Everybody is happier with a little more money, so don't be afraid to obtain wealth; it is of God.

The day I read in the Bible; money answers all things I screamed! I screamed because, for so long, people taught money is the root of all evil. Not true. The love of money is the root of all evil; however, cash is necessary for you and me to make an impact in this world. You may have extensive knowledge about a subject and have the answers, but because your finances do not allow you to be in a specific arena, or to run in one circle of influence no one will listen. However, men with millions have rambled themselves into positions of power. So much power they make life or death decisions concerning people they have never met.

Increase your financial stability. Since I am writing this book during quarantine, I have taken the opportunity to do some things to increase my financial security. I am taking some classes that will allow me to create income wherever I am. I have written this book, and I'm working on another. I have started Inspired 2 Live, my podcast on Anchor.fm. You can never go wrong when you bet on you. The most significant investment you can make is in yourself. There are limitless possibilities when you are the boss. Your ideas are worthy of being heard and will draw attention. Think like a boss, behave like a boss, be a boss.

My definition of Boss, B= Brave and blessed O= opulent S= successful and secure S= soul sister! Not only have I taken this time to do me, but I have also taken time to Team Build. Inspiring others is truly a gift. Watching others accomplish their goals makes me happy. As I am inspired and motivated, I pay it forward. There is no room for jealousy or competition in life. No two people have identical life plans. How can the two be compared or contrasted?

My mother is a QUEEN HUSTLER! Growing up, I remember helping her roll tamales, packaging dinner rolls, and plastic ware. She played piano for the church, sold dinners, made and sold lap scarves, Sarah Coventry Jewelry, Home Interiors, Avon, Mary Kay, and worked a full-time job.

She patterned the wellbeing of her household after that of the woman in Proverbs 31.

Pastor Carolyn L. Wilkins (Mom) was my first example of a God- fearing woman. I watched and learned how to take little entrust it to God and reap a greater blessing. Examples like this build us as people. Having our multiple streams of income is of God.

Financial stability requires wisdom in spending and giving. Mishandled finances are ADick. Breaking the aDicktion of financial instability requires getting to the root of it. The breaking involves a series of why's. The process is called Root Cause Analysis. We have lived with unanswered questions all our lives. Know a little kid? They ask a thousand and one questions until they are satisfied with the answer.

We must learn to question ourselves until the answers line up with the plan of God for our lives. If you lack wisdom, you can ask God, and he will give it to you. Trust in the Lord with all your heart and do not lean to your own understanding, in everything you do seek his ways, and he will guide you.

Chapter 11: Be Charitable with Wisdom

Deuteronomy 15:11

There will always be poor people in the land. Therefore, I command you to be openhanded towards your fellow Israelites who are poor and needy in your area.

Along your journey to freedom, do not forget the captives. Be aware of those around you in need of help. Be a Good Samaritan when you can. Refer to a capable resource if you cannot.

Never be too good or too busy to help

Whatever it is that tugs at your heartstrings do it. Look into tangible ways to be a part. It is vital that you do not give so much that you have nothing left. I am guilty of it. It is crucial that you not allow people to guilt you into giving. We all know financial naggers. They can beg the socks off your feet before you even know you have taken them off. There is a Dick going around now that believes it is ok to live free. You know that one that lives with your cousin rent free? He has access to all the things she works so hard to provide for her children, even with some authority. Lil Mike cannot even have his friends over to play the new 2k20 because Bae and his boys have the game system on lock. Foolishness I say pure foolishness. Having a mate does not require you pay for him. Say what you say, but if everything is in your name and paid by you Sis you are paying Dick. In some states this type of relationship is illegal. I am just saying. Impressive or Prompted giving will not land you in the bigger blessing pool. Thankfully, blessings are not given by lottery. We often laugh at people that get caught up in Ponzi scams. We fail to recognize the fact that sometimes we are in Ponzi's ourselves. I was one of those who jumped in the $100 lines for the offering. Admitting that often it was not just for the need of a blessing; it was to show I could give this $100 too. Money has been ADICK in churches. I gave an offering in Sunday school tithe in regular service an offering at the four o'clock program and another offering at the 7:00 PM concert.

At no point has God commanded me to give until I could see no money. I will not get off into the whole tithes & offering issue here;

however, I will say use wisdom in giving. Unsanctioned giving will cause a curse upon your finances. An immediate evil, as soon as you leave, that gaslight will remind you, Sis, you needed gas, and you just gave your gas money away. That is a curse. Your giving can not exceed your ability to live. Doing this makes you a blessing in one place and a burden in another. The blessings of the Lord make us rich and add no sorrow. Nobody is born a perfect manager of money. It takes time and wisdom to develop such a gift. Be wise with what you have, and much more will be added.

I make no apologies for the fact that your balls aren't big enough to handle my personality

~Pixie~

Chapter 12: Make no apology for choosing you.

Never feel guilty again for buying yourself a pair of shoes. How many shoes have you bought for people who walked away without thanks? Never again will you feel alone because people have walked away. You now have tools that will help you get over it. Make no apology for saying yes to yourself and no to Dick. Any person place or thing that does not want to see you happy and full is a Dick in your life. Make no apology for moving on. Seasons change, and so do relationships. Letting go may be the energy it needs to become a better relationship. Live your life, enjoy and never say I am sorry for being me again. It is when you live in joy; you find the strength to overcome every obstacle that stands in your way. When you make no apologies, you are free to live in abundance promised to you. No place in the plan of life concerning you was there ever design for failure. However, there is an alternative plan if a failure should occur. Do not be afraid to make mistakes.

Mistakes are your opportunities to improve yourself and prove to yourself that you can win. Your mistakes are the opportunities God takes to show you how much he cares. Make no apologies for wanting the best not only for yourself but for all those attached to you. Make no apologies for making yourself a priority. How can you contribute 100% to a situation when you are operating at 0% in real life? You are so tired you cannot pay attention. The improper diet causes you to lack strength, so you are a weak. Fatigue sets in at the worst moments. What good are you to the world when you are no good to yourself? Self-care is not a sin. It is a requirement for fulfillment of your assignment. Break the aDicktion of placing you last. Mark yourself essential because you are.

The ruby is the most valued colored gem. It is a geological wonder because of its composition and location. In the makeup of the Himalaya Mountains, there are slates of marble where ruby is naturally cultivated and protected. Most colored gems contain iron and other elements that enhance and increase the brilliance of their color. They need help being brilliant. The ruby is not so. It needs none of these elements to make it beautiful and valuable. No additives naturally worth it.

The darker the ruby, the more valuable the stone. Lighter ruby though still costly, is not of the same quality or esteem of the darker.

When I discovered these facts about the ruby, I got a revelation as to why Proverbs 31 likens a woman's worth to a ruby.

The more we go through and endure, it works out the unnecessary elements within us as we allow ourselves to purge the devaluing items our value increases, and the demand for women of our stature increases.

One day I sat down and did a self-appraisal. I looked at my progress in a few different areas of my life from an appointed date to present. In performing that appraisal, I discovered some people, places, and things I no longer had a vacancy for. These nouns had occupied rent-free space in my heart and mind far too long. Their occupancy was making it impossible for beneficial nouns to move in.

My appraisal revealed the visual evidence of my obedience to the will of God for my life. It further revealed that God had not aborted the plan for my life. He still finds me valuable, worthy, and the one selected for this assignment. I discovered that I have equity with God, and with equity comes a return.

No longer do you have to live in deficit because of past mistakes, bad choices, or failed attempts. You have experienced an element purge.

Some unnecessary things are far removed from you, and your value has increased.

Being bright and flashy in its season is acceptable and expected. However, as you mature, so should the brilliance of your color and shine.

My favorite comedian, the Queen of Comedy, in my opinion, Sommore, gave me life in her special, Chandelier Status. A fancy lamp is beautiful in the scheme of decorating. A chandelier, on the other hand, has a timeless beauty. Even after it has aged, it can be rewired and still give off brilliant light without losing its original beauty. Like the ruby, chandeliers are not mass-produced or mass duplicated. The valuable ones are rare and desired.

You must understand the value God has placed on you as a woman. No matter what society says about you, God declared you good. He created you fearfully and wonderfully in his image and likeness. God even though us worthy to partner with him in this thing of life and vision.

Make no apology for choosing you >>>Breaking the Chain of Codependency<<< 4 Major Links of the Codependency Chain Quiana R. D. Davis, MA, LLPC

Behavior Interventionist & Organizational Consultant Divine Mind Consultation Services Unclear and Inconsistent Boundaries Create and keep healthy boundaries with people that depend on you. Just because you love or care for someone does not mean you want to become the strength that enables their weaknesses. Whether it be your children, spouse, family members, or close friends, all relationships require boundaries. Think about it; if traffic had no signals, signs, or pavement markings, driving would be chaos. Use this metaphor when navigating your interpersonal relationships, knowing that without structure, they too are bound to crash.

Keep it "A Buck" (100% Real)

Do not bite your tongue. Speak the truth, no matter the case. Of Course, you can consider the delivery of your words to soften a blow, but somethings have no sugar coat. Plus, sugar is not sustainable; it melts in water, heat, and under pressure, and things just get sticky. Instead, tell those who overly rely on you the ugly truth. You do not want your words to be taken out of context and the receiving partner to misconstrue what could change their life.

Independence = InnerPeace

A lot of times, we cling to the things that hurt us the most. We tend to very loyal to our aDicktions. We do so because, on a personal level, there is a fear of abandonment and, ultimately, of being alone. As humans, we are hardwired for connection and a sense of community. If we have endured hostile relationships that have taught us that "any attention is good attention," we are especially prone to this shared co-dependent trait. We must remember this for those who are unhealthy, depending on us as well. Chances are the person that manifests most of the time is not the person who drew you in. It is usually a romanticized version of who they are or the person they show us in the "honeymoon phases" of the relationship. We cannot let our anxiety of isolation influence the way we interact with this person and create a mindset where we eventually share their negativity. If positive vibes are not a norm for this person, then breaking this link is healthy for your sanity-Ain't nobody got time for that.

Do You, Boo!

Stop worrying about what people think of you. You will never be able to please everyone. No matter how wonderfully you execute something, someone will always have something to say. The sooner you can accept this, the better off you will be. When we become consumed with "reading minds," we do so based on our insecurities. We take what we have been most self-critical about and magnify it from a place of assumption. This type of self-defeating behavior can create negative self-talk that is driven by anxiety.

Accepting ourselves for fearfully and wonderful creation, God has called us to starts when we increase our positive self-image and protect ourselves. This strategy, in part with a strong sense of confidence in our ability to say, "no" works as a magic formula for being unapologetically unique. Do you, boo!

Though not an exhaustive list of the links that create the chain of codependency, these four links can be the first steps to forming new habits that can set you free from its enslavement.

Jeremiah 29:11-13

I know the Plans I have for you declares the Lord plans to prosper you and not to harm you plans to give you hope and a future. Then you will call on me and come and pray to me, and I will listen.

———————⟨∞∽⟩———————

Knowing that the plan for you from conception was for success should make your heart sing. It is good news that the creator had an idea for you despite the circumstances of your birth or the conditions in which you lived. The plan concerning you has always been one of hope and a successful future. Do not apologize for walking in the fullness of what God intended for you. Live your best life, and do not go back and forth with anybody. It is your right to live free and delivered from aDicktions of all types. Live Free!

About the Author

Terra Vonesheia Riley M.C.E is a native of Saginaw, MI. She is a resident of Lansing MI and employed with Lansing School District at Everett High School. Terra is a proud mother and cherishes creative times with her children. She is known and loved for her comical way of teaching practical lessons. Transparent and real is how she believes everything should be taught.

As a singer/songwriter she has shared national platforms with many and as an artist herself. Terra has competed on the gospel artist talent search platforms of both INSP and BET. Her gifts have made room for her to work with Holland Dozier and Holland, Vickie Winans, Cherelle, Gee Pierce, Pam & Dodi, the late MC Breed and many more.

God is awesome in me! There is nothing that has happened in my life that I do not clearly understand is an Act of HIS Grace and Mercy toward me.

Terra proudly serves as a part of the Transforming Life Church Ministries family, pastored by Pastor William and Dr. Laura Brown of Saginaw, MI. She is a Masters graduate of ARM Bible Training Institute Midland MI.

www.ingramcontent.com/pod-product-compliance
Lightning Source LLC
LaVergne TN
LVHW051202080426
835508LV00021B/2761